The Real Bitches of New Jersey

by
Cathy Comora & David Comora
(Bitch Whisperers Extraordinaire!)

www.therealbitchesofnj.com
Publisher: Magical Genie, LLC.
Parsippany, NJ 07054
The Real Bitches of New Jersey
ISBN-13: 978-0-692-08268-3
Printed in China

We'd like to thank all the owners of the wonderful bitches and studs featured in this book, and acknowledge a special thank you to: Ed Kirchdoerffer and Dianne Ochiltree for their professional advice; Vince Gargiulo for his Photoshop skills and tremendous generosity; Allie Comora & her husband, Emily Comora, Mary Comora, Scutcharoo Comora, Jeanne Corcoran, Denise Diamond, Brent MacPhail, Tom Matrullo, and Richard Yorkowitz for their contributions and support. Thank you, Arlene Pearlman, for your keen wit and unwavering belief in this project.

A hearty tail-wag to Terry's Pet Stop in Morris Plains, NJ, for hosting The Real Bitches of NJ photoshoot!

Photos by: Renato Sexias, Shutterstock
Palisades Amusement Park Historical Society

Magical Genie

Having lived in the great state of New Jersey for most of our lives, we know first-hand that Jersey is home to some of the bitchinest bitches in the world!

As bitch whisperers extraordinaire, we are blessed with the gift of interspecies communication and have assembled here, a selection of some of our favorite furry friends who best exemplify the Jersey attitude.

Everyone from Jersey knows -- you can take a bitch out of Jersey, but you can't take the Jersey out of a bitch!

Cathy Comora & David Comora

Featuring:

The Shore Scene
The Atlantic City Scene
The Music Scene
The Mob Scene
The Food Scene
The Townie Scene
The Singles Scene
The Stray Scene

I'm from the Garden State

You got a problem with that?

Bitch: A Female Dog

Son Of A Bitch: A Male Dog

The Shore Scene

I'm down the shore!!!

I Caught Crabs

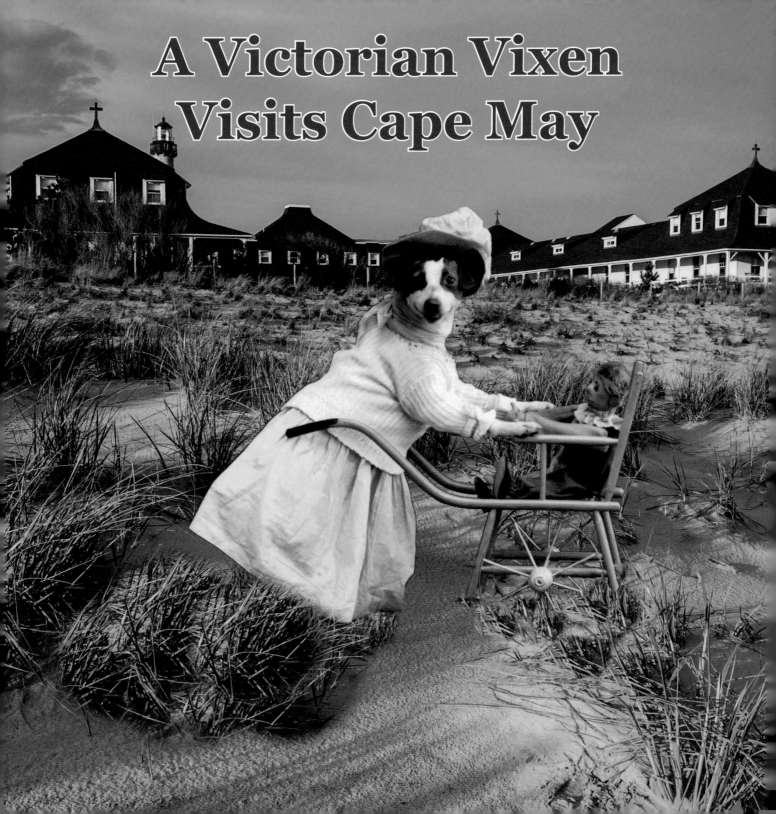

A Victorian Vixen Visits Cape May

Lookin' Pretty in Surf City

Naughty Beach Badge Dodgers

"I'm over 21 in bitch years!"

Bitches Night Out!

Tilly tones her tail

in preparation for
The Atlantic City Booty Pageant

The Board Game Bitch

Albina

(wife of the famed board game stud)

"The Real Salt Water Taffy Story"

Dog Fussy Magazine gives it 4 Wags!

Rover Ebert says: "Trust me, you don't want to know..."

Ruff night in AC

The Music Scene

SPRINGERSPANIELSTEEN

BUDDY
and the
ASBURY
WEIMARANERS
Contains the #1
hit single
Hearts
of Bone

HYDRANT
MUSIC INC.

Live at the

St. Bernardsville Bowl

Blonde Rockbitch

OL' BLUE BALLS

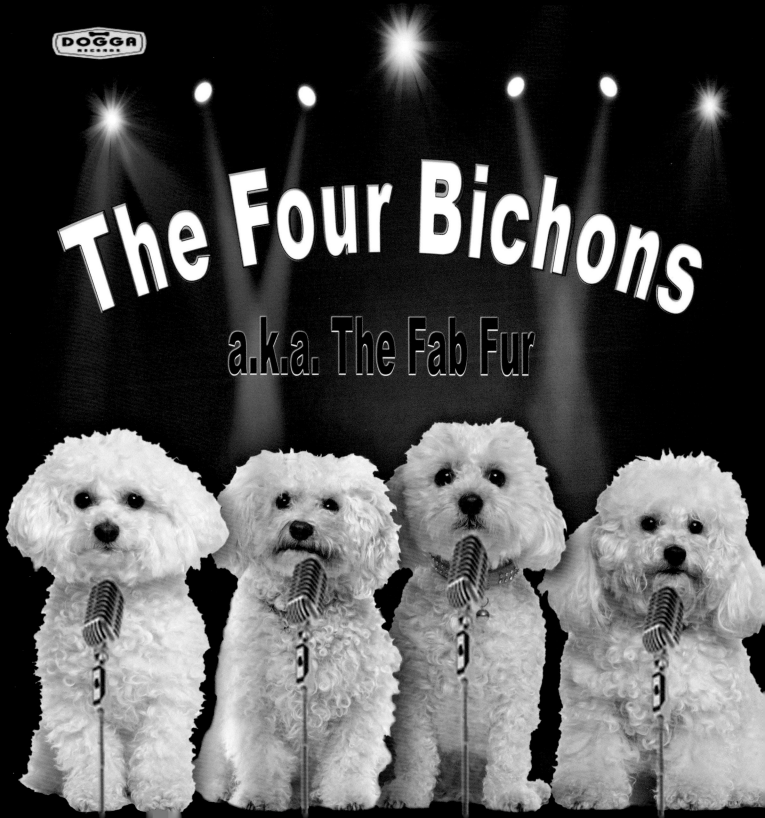

A Fur Out Funkadelic Fan From Fairlawn

Mob Bitches

The Singing Sopranos

Big Pussycat

Fuhgeddaboudit?

Funny how, bitch?

The Food Scene

Jersey Fresh

Mindy likes her bagels

with a schmear

Nothing could be finer

than eating at a diner
at 2:00 in the morning

North Jersey

Gimme the Taylor Ham, egg & cheese on a buttered roll

The Jersey Devil Dawg

Tell Sal I'm going to pick up the cannoli

The
Townie
Scene

Liberty State Park Selfie

Jersey City

The Blairstown Bitch

Big-Haired Bayonne Bitch

Rockin'
the
Jersey
Poof
Puff!

The Howling Hounds of Howell

Peapack & Gladstone

Lost Bitch

**If found, please return to:
the Conehead family of Paramus, NJ**

High Point State Park

Sussex

Bettylou, the Cotton Candy Bitch

Maria has a hankering for Chicken Piri Piri in Newark's Ironbound district

The Lizard of Menlo Park

The Real Butts of Butler

I got hitched to a bitch from Greenwich

THE WESTFIELD WATCHDOG

Coming

Soon

To

A

Theater

Near

You!

My grandmother was a watchdog

My mother was a watchdog

Now it's my time

BEWARE OF BITCH!

Zooing

Denville Dairy Dog

Relativity

Princeton

Hamilton, Lafayette, Washington AND Peggy

Morristown

Jersey bitches are sexy and they know it!

Jersey bitches are so hot,

I'm schvitzing!

Red Hot Jersey Tomato

Summer Jersey Girl

aka Bitch in Heat & Humidity

The Jersey Jerk

Bow Chicka Bow Wow!

Jersey bitches are always

ready to go out for a good time!

Baby Got Tail

Someday my fireman will come...

Stormy loves males blessed with long tails

Think Jersey bitches ain't got no class?

Youse are just jealous!
Jersey bitches rule!

"Don't be Farty At the Party"

Pia parties to The Real Bitches' song

Glory Days

The Jersey Slide

Jersey bitches be like:

Don't make me take my hoops out!

Jersey bitches have sass!

"Bye, Felicia!"

Soccer mom's advice:

"Bite his ball!"

Looking Fierce

Jersey Bitcholicious

Rich Bitch

Bark Obama visits New Jersey to save the Affordable Tongue Care Act

The weiner-dog

tweets a selfie to the real bitches of NJ

I am serious, Caesar!

If you put this on Facebook,
you are a dead dog!

Let your fun flag fly in Jersey!

Bitch Power

The Spirit of Jersey

Jersey Strong

The End!

Wherever she'll wander,
wherever she'll roam,
a Jersey bitch
will always
jughandle home.

Bios

Cathy Comora

Photo Credit: Kate Thomas Wood

Cathy is the creator/writer/designer of The Real Bitches of New Jersey.

Cathy dabbles in comedy writing, has written skits for local sketch comedy groups, and was nominated for a Louie Award for humorous greeting card writing. She is also the author of *The Real Bitches of Sarasota, Happy Birthday, Princess!* and *Birds in Bras: Breasted, Chested, Boobies & Tits.*

She has worked as an interpreter for the deaf and as a television publicist.

David Comora

Photo Credit: Emily Comora

David (writer/designer), Cathy's brother, is a lifelong New Jersey resident and dog lover. He and his wife Mary are the proud adoptive parents of Chester, a Plott Hound who was rescued from a shelter in North Carolina.

David toils in various media formats and directed the NY Emmy-Nominated documentary: *Palisades Amusement Park, A Century of Fond Memories.*